Conquering

Amy Morgan

Presentation by *BookLeaf Publishing*

Web: www.bookleafpub.com

E-mail: info@bookleafpub.com

ISBN: 9789357615525

First edition 2022

ACKNOWLEDGEMENT

Thank you to my dad and sister for their never wavering support. Also, thanks to everyone I have encountered who has shaped my life in some way, you have made me who I am, and I am grateful.

PREFACE

Delving into the mine of my mind, I hunted for peace. Taking wanders into nature inspired words to flow from me that I captured beneath the clouds. These honest thoughts transformed themselves into these poems that enabled me to reach an inner equilibrium.

Capturing

They tumble out of me
These words
Formed on my lips
Without effort
I have no influence
Over my beliefs
The core energy that
Radiates within
I attempt to capture it
Lure it in
To train and earn its trust
Prove I can

Exhausting

I don't honour how much I've gone through
This turmoil, this process
Headstrong determination
Never failing urge to push onwards
It's exhausting
Exhausting relying on myself
Knowing the danger
Experiencing it first-hand
Explanations knife my heart
I relate

The simple words of inpatient unit
Create an attack on my conscious
Surrounded by broken devils
Fragments of myself
Unable to cope
I want to run away

Oblivious to how much damage I did
Unaware of how lucky I am to be here
Blinded to how easily it could have gone badly
Been the end

I was balancing between the living and dead
Half of each

Willing to swing towards the afterlife
Ready to fling myself in front of traffic
Despairing
Scrambling to find a foothold
Anything to grab
To cling to
To save myself from the drop

But I fell

Wallowing

When the lights are extinguished
I am left alone in my own company
My mind follows the darkness
Wallowing into my past
Experiences I have yet to accept
Experiences I don't want to make real
But I must

For they lay deep within me
Dormant until awoken
A fiery vengeance
A reminder of my sacrifice
A scar on my subconscious
Interrupting regular function

I flail
Falling and falling
Gaining speed with no destination
A bottomless pit

I dig
Scraping at the sides
But there is no final finish
No accepted end
No respite

Erasing

Doubting myself
Going over my thoughts with Tipex
Willing them to be non-existent
They are written in permanent marker
Leaving a stain
I can't scrub away

Snapping

Urges drive their blades into my head
Desperate for me to start pretending
A little never hurt anyone they whisper
Wrapping themselves round my common sense
I am cocooned.

Lost touch with reality
Try to scream
Any noise muffled
Keeping myself together,
Only just.

A public place
Facing this challenge of my own creation
My decision with no one to blame,
Making it worse.

Mind lashing out at itself
Unable to do anything right
Just wrong
Wrong and disgusting,
Horrifying myself.

I want there to be no option off the table
No choice I would turn down from fear

But embracing them all with open arms isn't
simple
Trialling myself
Going against the current
Preventing myself getting swept along by
thoughts
Holding onto a branch
Wary of it snapping
And my effort being swept away
Drowned

Redefining

I have altered my measurement of success
Redefined my standards
Not written in permanent ink
But in pencil
Knowing they will alter as life alters
Fluid instead of unwavering
I have learnt that that having a life is more
rewarding
At least more than being restricted by my
restricting

Being

Gazing at the sun
This ball of fiery mass
That we time ourselves by
Place limits
Restrictions
Conditions
Upon our actions
Depending on it
This power it holds
Bewitching

Everyone entranced by the moon
Waning and waxing
The sun is a constant
Projector of our trajectories
We live and learn and love
Under its beams

Its ability to make or break a day
Its control over our mood, our emotions
The centre of our solar system
The centre of our survival
It will walk with us always

A glimmer of hope
Cast out in rainbow clouds
A signal, a sign of blessing
Radiating joy and hope
For when you fear all is lost

Winter nights draw in
Bringing blackout curtains
Smothering our fiery queen
Stifling the laughs
As the leaves turn auburn
Falling at our feet
Their crisp crunch deafening
In the silence

Empty parks, abandoned sports
Everyone turned internal
Barricading themselves in
For fear the frost could freeze fun
And the waiting begins
Waiting for the sun
To scoop us up into her rays
Thraw our frozen happiness
Release us to the world

Bruised from our harsh winter
Her golden warmth a reminder
We are alive
We have survived

Fleeing

Sprinting
Stumbling
Running
Fleeing
Crawling
Escaping
Flying halfway round the world
Running
Hunted

Desperate to escape,
By any means.

Longing to leave it behind,
Chasing nothing
Fearing the past
But there is one thing I can't lose
No matter how fast I run;
My mind.

It catches up with me
And trips me up.

Stumbling

Obstacle course stages
Slamming into me
Barely caught my breath
Before I'm thrown into it again
The same reps, the same actions
As I've been instructed to do
With as much effort as I desire

Can only be given so much advice
Guided through the basics
Let the reins loosen
Gaining trust, gaining momentum
Then the reins fall off
I stand in my own feet

Stumbling into reality
The real world greeting me
With its unavoidable bumps
Some reps are missed accidentally
Some skipped with intention
A life written out by rules
My restricted way of living
Familiar with regulations set in stone
Usually by myself
Usually getting less and less

More dramatic, more perilous
As I waste away and give up by giving in
Giving up is as hard as fighting it
A tug of war with no winners
Checkmate against myself
No finish line

Divided focus
Fading away
Until I get retaught
How to behave
How to care for myself
Basics of living even a child would know
Trusting their instinct
As I betrayed mine
Now it refuses to return
My hope lingers

Wishing

Lashing out
Sharp tongue
Cutting those
Who care
Loved ones
Saving me
Supporting me
I turn against them.

Hoping to
Remove the blockage of unwanted emotion I
don't want to claim but end up owning
And it floods me.

There is no land above water
No safe place to retreat to
I am surrounded
Trapped in a hailstorm of my own creation
Accessing an unwanted element of myself
This twisted side
It punishes me
For looking after myself
Making me wish I just gave in
Wishing for some kind of peace
I've been at war for years

And no treaty has been forged
Battles killing off both sides

Which will more be left of?
Which shall I begin to rebuild?
Is there even hope of rebuilding myself?

Unravelling

One imperfection
One snag in a pristine blanket
Intact apart from one loose thread
One I can't help but tug at
Unravelling my whole life
Yanking it harder initially

Then it begins to disintegrate
In my hands
Faster than I can control
Out of my depths
In a puddle of thread
That was once my life

Plunging

Inky depths lap around my head
I break the surface
Gasp
A single breath to last
Whilst I plummet back below
Choppy waters hold me
I fight back
Paddling constantly
No rest
Just to get above it
Breathe in
Before plunging again
Barely time to situate myself
Salty tang of tears
The lack of air
Constrained chest
A lifeboat on the horizon
Must wait here
Just keep paddling
Just don't give in
Stay strong
Safety will be here soon

Overthinking

Every move
Every moment
Dissected

What I did
What I didn't
Analysed

Every piece
Every choice
Reflected

What I could have
What I should have
Regretted

Suffering

Was I being too rash
How long do I have to undo this
Will I undo this
Am I giving in
I honestly have no clue
Being drawn out
Each limb torn, opposite directions
Loops in my head
I spin

Not wanting to commit
Wondering what will happen
How much influence I have over it
If I need to talk
If it will cause more problems
If it could open the door
I shut

Firmly closed as it was best for me
Is that selfish
I can't even imagine what she's going through
The loneliness
Isolation
Dark cave
Dripping tears

Running in torrents
Carving out space
To further retract into

Whilst I sit above
Laughing, living, loving
Being free
Wind in my hair
Her in a tornado.

Guessing what people will say
When approached for advice
They don't know all the sides
Barely I even do
Subconscious formed a curtain
Swept under past suffering
Protecting myself

I am surprised
To hear things that happened
For me it is just a gap
Time jumped forwards
I gaslight myself
Frantically on fire
Ashes to ashes

Drifting

Floating upon clouds
Scurrying across the land
No specific place or calling
Just paddling in the wind
Drifting away
My thoughts tangled in their trails
Tied to earth with my physical form
I have a soul that is unanchored
It soars above me
Willing me to fly

Disguising

Storm approaching
Chaotic waves
Gathering energy
All waiting for the break
A crash of thunder

Yet this must be masked
Draw down the blinds
Board up the windows
Hide the soul
Disguise the fear

Distract with games
Snuggle on down
Pretend you're away
Away somewhere safe
Somewhere safe from yourself

Where can your safe space be
When the danger is within?
A Labyrinth of emotion
Plonked in the centre
No maps, rely on instinct
Tainted with fear

Determination shouts up
Aiming for the front stage
Your outward appearance
Calm to be seen
Lying on the front line

For you are over it now
Want it forgotten
Banished from memories
No longer linked
With who you are
Enjoy the moment
Even with fear.

Breaking

Want to ask why
Want to scream and cry

A torrent of tears, woes
All flooding out

The dam may break
Unable to take another wave

I may break
I may have already broken

Aching

Stripped from my control
Situations that I can't snack in
Too exposed to ask for more
Deep belief to conform to the expectations
The reality of my illness
Desperately attempting to shake it off
Its claws dig deeper
As though tearing them out
Would leave a hole in my heart
And I'd bleed to death

Rooted so deeply
A solid oak centre
I leant against for too long
Realisation it wasn't normal
Bounces off my blindfolded self
Hunger was part of me
I felt something
This constant prick
An aching soul
Dragging my body through a life
I wasn't committed to

Facades starring in my own story
My protagonist a constant role

The painted picture-perfect smile
Fooling friends and family alike
Their needs over mine
The divide of time unbalanced
Hanging in a precipice of my own making
Solving others' problems
Reluctant search for my own solution
Brush off the concern

My anguish
That this leeching mechanism
I latched onto
Drained the essence of me
Away before my eyes
Loath to acknowledge it
Realising its presence
Never naming it
Even now

I don't recognise how entangled it got
How dangerous it became
How lucky I am to be alive
For I'd have given myself days
Before it pulled my trigger
Or drove my own hand to it

Pondering

Axis tilted
Feeling a bit off
No major cause
Just underlying emotion
Maybe exhaustion
Busy days
Thinking constantly
Pondering the universe
Subconsciously wondering
At the ways
It dictates actions
No rhyme or reason
Changing seasons
Flowing in a pattern
Repeating through years
But today I feel disconnected
Swung out across the poles
Yearning for an explanation
When often there is none
Generated from a build up
Mini events causing a big reaction
Waiting from afar
Stalking its prey:
My vulnerable soul

Searching

Seedlings power through
Searching for sunlight
Bending and twisting
Environment influenced growth
Each leaf is identical to the passer-by
No one notices their individuality

Why are we so obsessed
With yearning to be the same
When even nature breaks that pattern

Hurtling

Unable to comprehend how much life it takes up
All my ambitions, dreams, goals
Squashes them into boxes
Ashamed to see the light
Cloaked from my conscious
I am led on autopilot
Driving me further and further away from my
authentic soul
Lost on the highways of my mind
Unable to get back to the steering wheel
Chaos crashes
Consequences thrown out the window
Scrambling for the handle
Yanking it
Trying to escape
Hurtling at top speed
Towards my top fear
Being unable to control myself
Autonomy an honour
That I am deprived of
For good reason
For achievement
For I am unworthy
Roundabouts with no exit
Loops of patterns

I give up
Release control
It is too hard now
But then I take my test
New teachers
Fresh lessons
I sit down
Drive away
But it still grabs the wheel
Determined to crash
Avoid my destination
With all its willpower
But it underestimated
My eagerness
This pain
This journey
Will not be repeated
I will get there
Settle into my paradise
And destroy any maps it made
No return routes

www.ingramcontent.com/pod-product-compliance
Lightning Source LLC
La Vergne TN
LVHW010934200726
843509LV00013B/2208